WHAT MA...
ME H...

Hann...

In aid of
BBC
Children
in Need

WHAT MAKES ME HAPPY?
A CENTUM BOOK 9781910114360
Published in Great Britain by Centum Books Ltd
This edition published 2014
1 3 5 7 9 10 8 6 4 2

In aid of
BBC
Children in Need

© BBC 2007 Reg. charity England & Wales no. 802052
and Scotland no. SC039557

Centum Books Ltd, Unit 1, Upside Station Building, Solsbro Road, Torquay, Devon, UK, TQ2 6FD
books@centumbooksltd.co.uk
CENTUM BOOKS Limited Reg. No. 07641486
This book is published by Centum Books Limited on behalf of Hanni Blaskey and in aid of BBC Children in Need. Hanni has sourced and compiled the book's content. Centum is merely publishing the book and has not had any involvement with sourcing or compiling the book's content. All comments, quotes and other content have been supplied to Hanni by celebs whom Centum understands are happy to be involved in this project and who have contributed their own original content which expresses the celebs' own views.

A CIP catalogue record for this book is available from the British Library
Printed in United Kingdom

£2 from the sale of each book will benefit The BBC *Children in Need* Appeal
(charity number 802052 in England & Wales and SC039557 in Scotland).

Contents

I decided to raise money for BBC Children in Need because I was watching it 2 years ago and I saw how many children needed help, in so many different ways. I realised how lucky I was and I decided to help.

My big idea was to make a book for BBC children in Need about what makes people happy. I have asked a variety of interesting and famous people to write or draw what makes them happy. All of the profits from the sales of the book will be donated to BBC children in need.

So, with a little help from my family and friends I tried to reach as many famous people to write what makes them happy.

I hope by reading this you can see how so many different things can make people happy.

I started trying to collect the letters by waiting outside a music studio to wait for any famous people who were there. Little Mix then came out and at first, I was very nervous above approaching them, but I knew I had to! They were very friendly and they were the first people to be in my book.

I then took every opportunity to ask my friends to ask any famous people they might meet. Of course, I also started to find my own ways to ask and meet people - including asking Dizzee Rascal in an airport! I also went to the strictly Come Dancing studio where all the stars were in the same room.

Everyone I've asked has been so helpful and I can't believe that I have collected over a hundred famous and interesting people! It's amazing to see what very different things make people happy.

I would like to thank everyone who has been involved, including my family, the celebrities and Mr Cameron for their contributions to this book.

I hope you have as much fun reading the entries, as i had collecting them.

Nanné Blaskey
x

5

1O DOWNING STREET
LONDON SW1A 2AA

4 July 2014

THE PRIME MINISTER

Dear Rick,

Thank you for inviting me to write the foreword for your book, 'What Makes Me Happy'.

I was particularly heartened to learn that your 13-year-old daughter, Hanni, has been the driving force behind such an excellent idea of delving into what makes people happy. Your collaboration with Children in Need to raise money for the causes they support is also highly commendable.

I launched the National Wellbeing Programme six months after the Coalition Government came in to office. I saw this as an important thing to do to gauge the nation's wellbeing. I wanted to know what mattered to people and what made people happy. Various groups of society took part in activities which would give a better idea of what was important to them. This programme has, since its launch in 2010, allowed both myself and the Government to gain a better understanding of how what we do impacts on people and understand what people are most concerned about; allowing us to ensure that our actions are as supportive and fair as they can possibly be.

On a personal level, my own happiness index is very easy to explain: it is all about my family. Whether it is the everyday routines I go through with Samantha and the children; taking my youngest daughter Florence to nursery; helping Nancy complete her homework; or watching Elwen play football and rugby, I am at my happiest when surrounded by those I love the most and enjoying quality time with them. Although, given my current job, that is not always easy, it makes the time I can spend with Sam and the kids, even more special.

I know that many people have offered their own personal accounts and expressions of what makes them happy for this tremendous book, and I am sure their insights will make for a great read.

This comes with my best wishes to you and Hanni for every success with the book.

Yours,

David

Andy Murray

Spending time at home with my girlfriend and our 2 dogs! I travel for 6 months every year and miss being with my dogs a lot. So much so that I have travelled with them to some tournaments! They don't care whether I win or lose. They make me smile everyday I spend with them.

Watching my dog Bitko eat ice cream makes me happy!!

John Bishop

9

Alex Ferguson

There are many things that make me happy. I've had a long and happy Marriage of 48 years to Cathy. we have 3 sons who are all doing well in their own right and have gifted us with 11 wonderful grandchildren. watching them grow up has been really exciting as you see the different personalities come out from them. I have been lucky well having some great friends and it makes me happy that a lot of them grew up with me and 3 of them were in nursery with me! On a professional note I was fortunate to manage two wonderful Clubs Aberdeen F.C. and Manchester United F.C. So all in all having great parents, School teachers and good coaches when I was a boy it has been a happy life

Yours

Alex. Ferguson

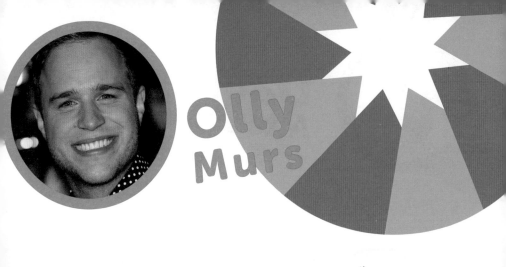

Olly
Murs

BEING AROUND MY FRIENDS AND
FAMILY IS WHAT MAKES ME HAPPY.
WITH ALL THE TRAVELLING
AND SUCH A HECTIC SCHEDULE NOW
I RARELY GET TO SPEND QUALITY
TIME WITH THEM SO WHEN I DO
I CHERISH IT.

David
Attenborough

The sun rising in the mountains makes me happy.

David Attenborough

Ideas line this book

Jack
Dee

12

Bass!

Lots of Bass!!!

DIZZEE RASCAL

Dizzee Rascal

Cerys
Matthews

What makes me happy?
You sing with me —
— the more the merrier —
i.e. a good ol' sing-song — lots of love
Cerys x

13

Little Mix

Perrie

What makes me happy...?

What makes me happy is waking up everyday knowing I do what I love for a living. I get to perform to thousands of people, and have amazing fans, I also love spending time with my loved ones. and Just chilling out.

Perrie ♡ x

Jade

WHAT MAKES ME HAPPY—
is seeing my friends and family when I haven't seen them in sooooooo long. Being in this industry (and having a family who still live up North) it harder to see them so when I do it amazing !!!

Jade
x

14

Leigh

Having girlie nights with my friends just like we used to do when we were younger and going to my mums with my dogs and seeing all the family on a Sunday! My mum makes the best roast dinner!

Leigh x

Jesy

being with my friends and laughing so hard that I slightly wet myself and my stomache feels allough its done about 900 situps also nandos :)

Jesy

Cliff Richard

SIR CLIFF RICHARD

I've visited many 'needy' places in our world and usually leave feeling depressed and helpless - so what makes me happy is to find that there are young (and older people too) who do care for those in need and actively do something to help!

Cliff Richard

Darcey Bussell

Sunshine,
Dancing,
Music and
Friends & family

Best wishes

Pixie Lott

Things that make me happy.....

Music   CATS

Friends

Family   Performing

Cookies   Holidays

smiles   partayz

Sunshine   Shopping

Percy Pigs loves Pixie Lott

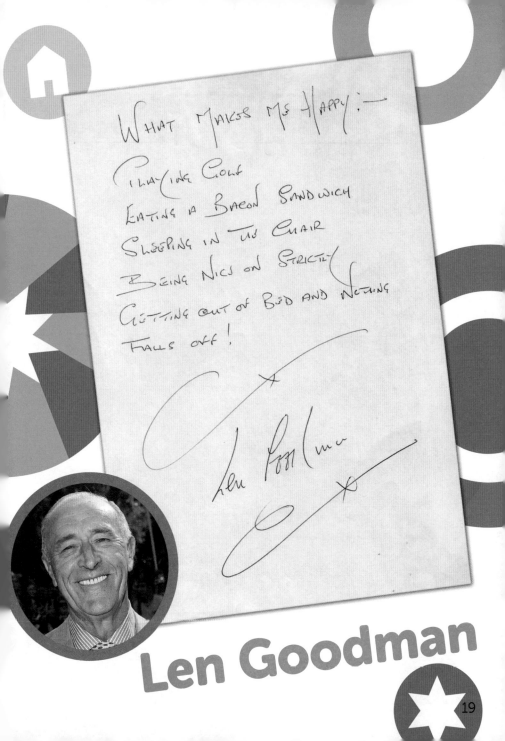

WHAT MAKES ME HAPPY :—

PLAYING GOLF
EATING A BACON SANDWICH
SLEEPING IN THE CHAIR
BEING NICE ON STRICTLY
GETTING OUT OF BED AND NOTHING
FALLS OFF !

Len Goodman

Len Goodman

Sarah
Duchess
of York

'Your eyes open and life is a fresh new day, the sunlight nudges through the curtains, suddenly excitement fills the room, another day begins. I do believe in fairies, I do believe in magic and when you blow on a dandelion, you will see the flight of the enchanted spreading their wings and disappearing off on their own journeys, just like you have today when you opened your eyes. Don't let the day go by without looking for fairies and magic.'

This makes me happy, as every day is therefore a day of exploration and adventure.

Good luck with your project and thank you for helping Children in Need.

Sarah, Duchess of York

What makes me happy is music!

Sophie
Ellis-Bextor

Roy
Hattersley

Dear Hanni
I had to e-mail you because my handwriting is so awful that
you would not be able to read a word.
I'm one of those lucky people who are happy all the time.
But some things make me especially happy.
Walking over the hills with my dog — Jakie, a white English
Bullterrier. Writing — not newspaper articles any longer
but books. Drinking tea. And watching old films — they call
them movies on the television — in bed, late at night.

Thank you for including me in your book.

Roy Hattersley

Omid Djalili

Ultimately what makes me happy in this crazy, hectic world of ours, is having a mind clear of worries where it has the freedom to express game changing thoughts like "Thank God watermelons don't grow on trees, otherwise if one fell on top of someone it could kill them!"

Actually having read that back it's probably best I keep my mind pre-occupied with work related matters. But ya feel me? ¨

Omid Dj

Rochelle Humes

Rochelle Humes
xxx

Marvi
Alaia-Mai
Family

Kiss

LOVE

Happy People

THE SATURDAYS

Gaby Roslin

What makes me happy? . . . .

My kids +
My Husband +
A lot both!

Gaby Roslin
xxx

What makes me happy my children
in the morning when they haven't woken
up enough to misbehave!

Michael McIntyre

Bear
Grylls

'Coming Home'

Bear

Jens
Lehmann

1. What makes me happy?.

- Eating chocolate
- Playing football and watching exciting games.
- Skiing
- Playing with my children!

J. Lehmann

Ed Miliband

My family is the most important thing in the world to me and spending time with my wife Justine and my boys, Daniel and Sam is what <u>always</u> makes me happy.

Daley Thompson

The 3 things that make me happiest are...

1. My 5 kids who give me the best reason ever to get up in the morning.
2. My friends, who accept me despite all my faults.
3. Sports, which we invented based on Utopian ideals.

And one more "with all its sham, drudgery and broken dreams it's still a world".

I hope this is what you're looking for.

Abbey Clancy

What Makes me happy
by Abbey Clancy

It makes me happy when other
people are happy
It Makes me happy seeing one
laugh and smile
It Makes me happy Seeing my
beautiful daughter and seeing
my husbands face in hers !!
Snuggling my little baby Makes
me happy watching her sleep
Seeing her playing hearing her
giggle
It makes me happy when I am
around my loved ones mum dad
brothers and sister and obviusly
being with my husband and baby
Music makes me happy
laughing makes me happy
All in All im a happy Person

27

Maureen Lipman

I believe that happiness comes as a result of submerging oneself in some other activity. Happiness is released like a kind of gas from a rock. So happiness is not something we are owed but something we earn. It comes about via certain rules followed unconsciously. If I master a few dance steps or watch an interesting programme whilst painting or decoupaging a box or a mirror or pack up and take a bag of clothes to a drop in-centre or sleep right through the night without waking, then I suddenly feel a sense of being entirely inside that speck of time and at peace with myself. That to me is happiness.

'I am not interested in the pursuit of happiness, but only in the discovery of joy.' - Joyce Grenfell

James
Morrison

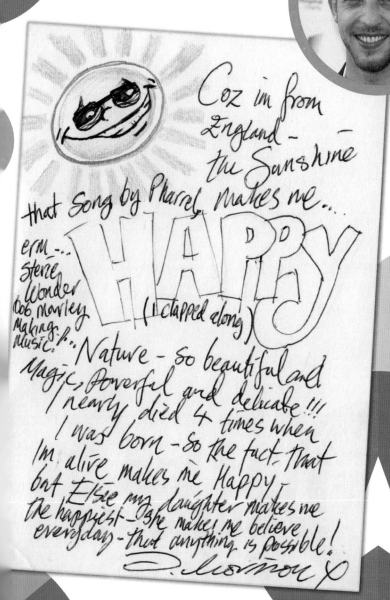

Coz im from England - the Sunshine

that Song by Pharrel makes me...

HAPPY (I clapped along)

erm... stevie wonder bob marley Making... Music!..

Nature - so beautiful and Magic, Powerful and delicate !!! I nearly died 4 times when I was born - So the fact that Im alive makes me Happy - but Elsie my daughter makes me the happiest - She makes me believe everyday - that anything is possible!

What makes me happy..... ♪♪ ♪ ♪

is dancing with my children! My
boys are 8, 9 and 11 years old
and they love to put some
great music on at home and
we boogie around - it makes
you feel great - and is a
lovely thing to do together.

Susanna Reid

Susanna Reid

Susanna Reid

Martin Clunes

What Makes Me Happy....?
My Clyesdales..!

Simon Mayo

really wild, crazy
stormy, tempestuous
out of control weather !

party on...
Simmmayo

Sunshine makes me happy.
I love cold winter days with a bright
blue sky and brilliant sunshine but I'm
happiest on a warm sunny summer's day.
If there's a cricket match nearby that's
the icing on the cake.
I also love icing on cakes......
Jim Carter. x

Jim Carter

Imelda Staunton

What makes me happy?
Walking very early in the mornings
during the summer with my little
dog .... either on the Heath or
by the Sea ..... heaven!
Imelda Staunton

Imelda
Staunton

Hugh Dennis

Dear Hamni

Here is a list of things that make me happy!

My wife

My Kids

Football.

A Football,

The sports section

A smile

Toast

A Good Joke

Nice weather

A seat outside the Pub.

Stay Happy

Hugh Dennis

X

Being silly, laughing and having no worries in the world. Being myself makes me happy. Just feeling free around people I love!! I love letting go!

Jessie J

Jessie J

Nigel Farage

Being with my four healthy children and thinking how lucky we all are compared to so many. This is a time to think about others less fortunate than ourselves.

Nigel Farage

34

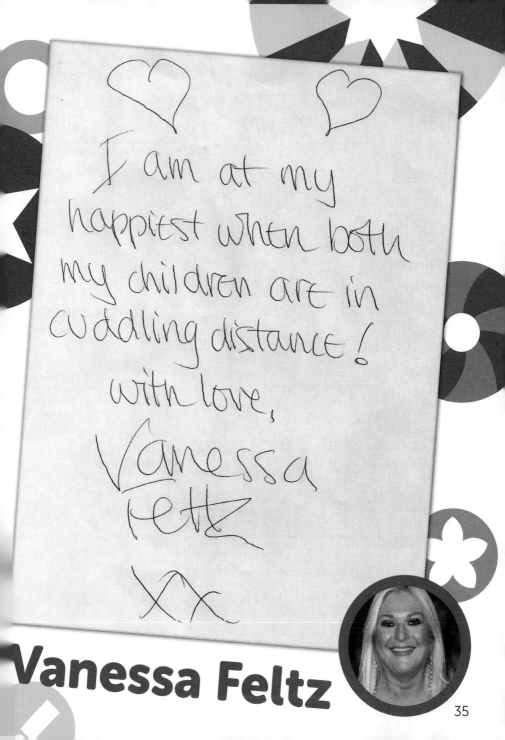

I am at my happiest when both my children are in cuddling distance!

with love,

Vanessa Feltz

xx

Vanessa Feltz

Denise
van Outen

"Notting makes me happier than spending time in my garden in the country with my daughter Betsy. We enjoy looking for the fairies that live at the bottom of the garden, making daisy chains in the summer and looking for acorns and chestnuts in the winter."

Denise Van Outen
x

Kimberley
Walsh

What makes me happy is .... spending time with my gorgeous nephew Billy.

Kimberley
xxx

Barney Harwood

Brendan Cole

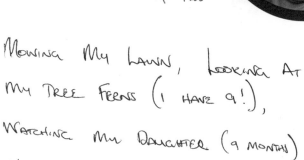

What makes me happy...

Mowing my lawn, looking at my tree ferns (I have 9!), watching my daughter (9 months) changing and growing and watching the All Blacks play Rugby!

Most things make me happy life is pretty good!

Brendan Cole.

Naga
Munchetty

Peaceful, Happy, Healthy—
          Family & Friends...
The Love of my Husband...
Affection from my Cats...
The Sun on my Face...
A Fabulous Golf Shot...
A Job Well Done...
        Love, Love, Love... x

          Naga xo

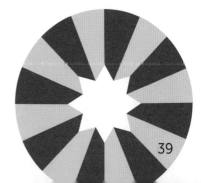

Clare
Balding

Walking my dog Archie every day. Whatever the weather, he makes me smile + we explore the world together.

Clare Balding

What makes me happy?

Spending time with Lisa and our children, laughing, sharing stories and having fun. That is what makes me really happy.

Will
Carling

Stacey Solomon

To Hanni!

Lots of things make me happy! But most of all making other people happy makes me happier! I love to give to others, and sing to people to make them happy! Giving, & doing for others is what makes me happy!

Lots of Love

Stacey Solomon
x

Russell Watson

Things that I like

Ray's of sunshine flickering though my bedroom curtains in the morning.

Blue skies, frost covered grass and the steamy breath blowing from my mouth like a cloud of smoke.

Different sized walking boots all covered in mud by the door, the smell of a log fire and laughter in the air.

The sound of rain pitter pattering on glass and watching my kids splash in puddles

Hot drinks and pies just before a big football game.

The way my gran used to smile and trips to the seaside.

I like all these things

Phil Watson

Julia Neuberger

What makes me happy is seeing my children happy, is a long swim in an empty pool, is driving towards our Irish house and coming over the crest of the hill and seeing the sea. What makes me happy is being able to give grants of money to destitute asylum seeker and to refugees to help with their education. What makes me happy is to feel that my congregation is in good spirits. What makes me happy is, on the whole, being alive and being able to do things.

43

What makes me happy is cooking Sunday Roasts and getting my whole family together.

Lots of Love
Louise ♡

Louise
Thompson

Katie Melua

What makes me happy is....

Great Poetry

lovely melodies

good books!

Sunny days.

Tasty Apples

gorgeous looking & sounding Guitars

Katie
xxx

Alan Titchmarsh

What makes me happy is – in every instance – anything that brings me closer to nature: walking in my wildflower meadow; boating on the river or sea; standing on top of a hill and looking at the view or examining closely the flowers of a bee orchid. Getting up close and personal with the natural world helps me to keep things in perspective and reminds me of my responsibility to it and the sheer joy and delight I get from it. And there is no better place than Britain to enjoy it!

Gary
Barlow

John McCririck

Happiness is being with your own devoted Booby, with our 3 Labradors and a cat, keeping healthy and going racing. Caring for others is also incredibly rewarding as is watching Jeremy Kyle and Deal or No Deal!! Life's best motto is 'work comes first — before family or pleasure — because neither is truly fulfilling if you're not working.' Stay happy, get a pet if possible, and share your good fortune and joy of life with all around you. Backing a big race winner also helps, so would Newcastle United winning anything and England regaining the Ashes. You're odds-on!

47

Adam Shaw

No more hair loss overnight.
Morning sun that's warm and bright Marzipan
and Pumpernickle, rice and baked beans.
That's my tipple
A crisp blue shirt
Slippers - warm and cosy
Toasted bread and melted butter
Easy mornings, Friendly people, cups of tea
And poetry better than this that scans and
Rhymes

PS: not sure how to spell pumpernickle.

Sol Campbell

My Wife
and kids

Melvyn Bragg

THE LORD BRAGG OF WIGTON

14. 3. 14

What makes me happy?
One sure thing is —
Listening to great Music.

God luck — Melvyn Bragg

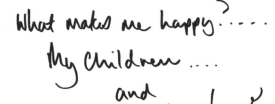

What makes me happy?.....
My Children ....
and
Shoes! love Myleene Klass

Myleene Klass

Richard Madeley

Being up early enough to see the sunrise over Talland Bay in Cornwall. Neatest thing to paradise on earth.

Richard Madeley

David
Garrett

30th March 2014
Miami

Life makes me happy!
Enjoying each moment, truely
living in it, and respecting time.
Life equals time, which we should
always value.
If you can succeed in this, you
will never regret anything.
Finding meaning in each moment
makes me happy.

Michael
Attenborough

"Being with my wife, two sons and new daughter-in-law; music, of all genres, that touches me emotionally; directing wonderful, truly collaborative actors, particularly in new plays and Shakespeare; humour that enables me to see the world anew; watching Chelsea play great football and win; losing myself in the natural world; reading a book that I can't put down; beautiful food; the English countryside in Spring; being near water; therapeutic massage; generosity of spirit; Christmas Eve; sunshine; thunder storms; being trusted; looking into Karen Lewis' eyes."

Michael Attenborough. C.B.E. D.L

Sam Bailey

Children in Need

What makes me happy ??

Watching my children
Playing and having fun
makes me happy 😊

lots of love
Sam Bailey x

Dame Shirley Bassey

Dame Shirley Bassey DBE

What makes you happy?

People smiling.

Dame Shirley Bassey

Paloma Faith

What makes me happy is the kindness of strangers.

Paloma Faith

Kevin
Pietersen

'What makes me happy is, waking up on safari away from the hustle & bustle of London city living!

Love *KP* 24

(KEVIN PIETERSEN)

Russell
Grant

What makes me happy is being by the seaside or a river and sitting back reading my favourite history and geography books.

Katherine Jenkins

Happiness is . . . .

Singing LOVE Wales Shoes

My Grandson Jac

Family

Home A.L.

Music Friends Girlie lunches

The Sea Gardens

Lily Rugby

Katherine xxx

Paul
McCartney

What makes me happy is to have a weekend off from my travels and concerts and spend it with family 1 love, to hear the noises in the kitchen as a meal is prepared and then my little grandson climbs on my knee and requests a bite of mine for every bite that 1 take. There's nothing better to enjoy than having my wife, kids and grandkids around on a lazy weekend.

Natascha McElhone

Work hard, expect nothing, celebrate !

Natascha McElhone

Baroness Lawrence of Clarendon

is Seeing
the smiling faces of young people who th
Stephen Lawrence trust has supported

Baroness Lawrence of Clarendon.

Paul Carrack

Lots of things make me happy, Sheffield Wednesday scoring a goal makes me behave like a complete idiot. My grandson (2 yrs) singing along to 'I've got a lovely bunch of coconuts' at the piano.

But something that really makes me happy is having a good old sing with my band and seeing the audience smiling and having a great time. It's the simple things.

59

The thing that makes me Happy is Riding my Bike around the world and the people you meet. "It's all about the people".

Big Love

2014.

~ xtt

Charley
Boorman

Gillian
Anderson

John
Suchet

Music, music, music. Beethoven above all others, but when he's not available, trad jazz. Strauss waltzes — anything with a tune.
And strictly in private, I'll take my trombone out of its box and play for hour after hour. Good thing only I can hear it!

John Suchet

Music, music, music. Beethoven above all others, but when he's not available, traditional jazz, Strauss, waltzes — anything with a tune. And strictly in private, I'll take my trombone out of its box and play for hour after hour. Good thing only I can hear it!

Peter
Andre

Lynda
Bellingham

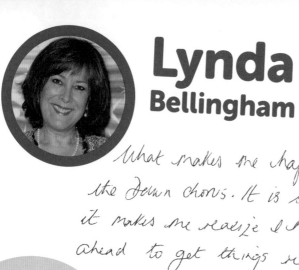

What makes me happy is hearing the dawn chorus. It is so full of hope it makes me realise I have another day ahead to get things right!

Good luck

Lynda Bellingham

Young People making music —

Barry
Manilow

Jasper Carrott

Labradors make me happy!
They're easy to beat at chess
and they're sucless when it
comes to knock, knock jokes

Knowing the ones I love
are healthy & happy

Lots of love
Barbara Windsor
X

Barbara Windsor

Uri Geller

URI GELLER ENTERPRISES

FOR Children in Need:

Being with my family makes me happy!

Walking with my dogs makes me happy!

Meditating and being a vegeterian makes me happy!

Much Energy!

Uri Geller

Rod Stewart

Many, many things make me happy. Life itself makes me happy. Being surrounded by my many children makes me ecstatically happy. Seeing my gorgeous wife's smile in the morning makes me happy. Teaching my boys how to play football makes me happy. Singing to lots of happy people makes me happy. Watching Celtic makes me happy. A nice cup of tea makes me uncontrollably happy. Many, many things in life make me happy, but I'm not happy all the time. Nobody is. But most of the time I'm blissfully happy and so I should be. I've led a very charmed life.

Gary Lineker

Walking my dog makes me happy. His utter joy at the word 'walkies' never diminishes.
Such enthusiasm for something so simple is strangely satisfying.

Being with the people
I love!

Jessie Wallace

Jessie Wallace

My beautiful family standing
by my side through every
event!

Never Give Up!

Nick Wallenda

Nick Wallenda

David
Seaman

WINNING MEDALS MAKES
ME HAPPY!!

Safe Hands

David Seaman

Grant
Shapps

The rare occasion
when I check my
diary and discover
there's nothing in
it for the next
hour!

Grant
Shapps

My house

Gareth Malone

Happiness is being true to myself, true to others and living with an open heart. Happiness is sturdy feet and open arms. Happiness is clean sheets and chocolate and kissing.

Will Young

Will Young

What makes me happy?

Lewis
Moody

Playing with these monkeys

Alex
Armstrong

Every morning. whatever mood they come bounding in, I am always so deliriously happy to see our children. Being with the family makes me blissfully happy

Sitting in the sun
and trying to
paint the view, or
possibly a person.

Boris
Johnson

Boris Johnson signature

Sharon Corr

Little things make me happy – singing along with the radio turned up in the car. Meeting my daughter to go shopping. Seeing Dundee Utd win with my husband.

x
Lorraine Kelly.

Lorraine Kelly

MUSIC MAKES ME

VERY

HAPPY!

CeeLo Green

Nick Grimshaw

GLASTONBURY

grimmy X.

Jeremy Vine

What makes me happy?

A poem written by my seven-year-old.

Finding out stuff I didn't know about Kings & Queens (I never listened to history in school).

Cycling downhill.

The opening bars of Honky Tonk Women.

Sitting in my tiny garden in London.

Friends, mainly.

You reading this.

Jeremy Vine
BBC Radio 2

Lynda La Plante

What makes me happy - Lynda laPlante CBE

When the sun shines I feel Happy.

Hearing children's laughteen is always a
wonderful tonic. If This book gives
'Children in Need' a sunny smile, THAT
would make me enormously happy.
                    Higher
Nothing lifts my heart than the sond
of Happy children.

Louis Walsh

Life MAKES me HAPPY
BECAUSE ...

I Love life

I love people (well! most of them!)

I love music (yes!)

and I like my friends (I HAVE SOME)

HAPPY is good !

Best wishes

Louis Walsh

P.S. Life is short too

79

Angel Blue

There's a brilliant part of the sky, that no one can deny... it's the place where angels fly smiling and happily they fly while watching over me. They listen while I sing All of Heaven smiles down on me Joyfully, thankfully, I raise my voice to Thee.
SINGING! That's what makes me happy.

SOPRANOS HAVE MORE FUN!

ANGEL BLUE

When one of my children walks through the door with a smile on their face!

Thomas Bjørr

Getting up early to walk to the village green to watch the sunrise, to meditate and to read. To write a list of things I was grateful for the previous day and to plan a wonderful day ahead, this is my perfectly happy start to my happy day.

Jeff Brazier.

Jeff Brazier

CREATING
MAKES
ME
HAPPY
& TAKING CARE
OF PEOPLE

Will.i.am

Aled Jones

FAMILY

Summer

Summer

love

Terry Wogan

The brilliant response of the British public to our yearly appeal on behalf of the country's underprivileged, sick and deprived children on BBC Children in Need. It's awesome, and makes me happy and proud to be part of an incredible appeal.

Brendan O'Carroll

4/7/2014

My Dog "NILES" Makes Me Happy!

Andrew
Lloyd Webber

My family, good wine, great musicals and my Turkish Van Cats.

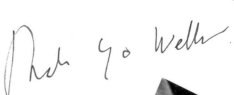

Michael Ball

Raindrops on Roses
Whiskers on Kittens
Bright Copper Kettles
Warm Wollen Mittens...

... Basically, if we want to,
we can set the whole of life
to music, which guarentees
everyone is happy.

Michael Ball

X

Sara Cox

Dancing round the kitchen to a good song ♪ on the radio 🎵 with my 3 gorgeous children ♥ and my lovely husband ♥ makes me very happy.

A strong cup of tea ☕, a lie-in, horse-riding 🐴, sunshine ☀ and my dog being daft all make me happy too.

♥ Sara Cox
xxx

MAKING A SNOOKER BREAK
OF ANYTHING HIGHER THAN FIFTEEN
AT THE RAC CLUB.

Don Black

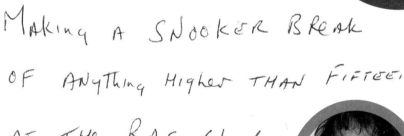

Don Black

Dermot O'Leary

GOOD QUESTION,

I'D SAY, QUITE A LOT, I'M A PRETTY
HAPPY PERSON.

BUT I LOVE BEING IN MY GARDEN
FIRST THING IN THE MORNING HAVING A
CUP OF GOOD COFFEE, WITH MY CATS
LISTENING TO LONDON WAKE UP.
SIMPLE PLEASURES

Tony
Blackburn

LOTS OF THINGS MAKE ME HAPPY, SPENDING TIME
WITH MY FAMILY, DOING MY RADIO SHOWS, PICKING THE
MUSIC FOR THE SHOWS I DO EVERY WEEK AND THE
THRILL OF A GOOD CHART RUN DOWN ON PICK
OF THE POPS!!. I ALSO LOVE TO SPEND A DAY
WATCHING CORONATION STREET AND CATCHING
UP ON EPISODES I HAVEN'T HAD TIME TO WATCH.
I KNOW THERE ARE LOTS OF OTHER THINGS THAT
MAKE ME HAPPY BUT THESE ARE THE ONES I CHERISH
THE MOST

Tony Blackburn

89

Elaine Paige

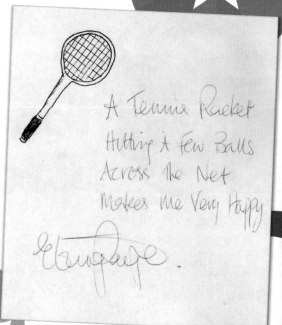

A Tennis Racket
Hitting A Few Balls
Across the Net
Makes Me Very Happy

Carl Hester

Watching my Battersea Rescue Dog changing
from Sad to Ruling the Roost.

P.S She originally wanted to eat them !!!

Carl Hester x x x

David Baddiel

Cats, football (some of the time — sometimes it makes me really unhappy), curry, sleeping. food, music, going on holiday, finding out that something I didn't want to go to has just been cancelled, a comfy pair of underpants, laughing and cats.

p.s. And my children. I have to say that

p.p.s. But they do. DAVID BADDIEL

Lee Westwood

SUNSHINE!

Laura Wright

The feeling
when you finish an
album, after you've
put so much creativity
into it...

The power we
can have by
working Together... (")

Living every day
as if it was
your last...

Laura Wright

x

2

ALL CHILDREN IN NEED ACROSS THE WORLD AND BRITAIN WISH YOU LOTS OF HAPINESS AND STAY STRONG

IVANOVIĆ B.

SAMSUNG

Branislav Ivanović

Mike
Bushell

"The thrill of trying a new sporting activity with friends or family for the first time, and laughing so much when at first, it catches us out."
Thanks Mike

Justin Rose

sunset family time, playing eating, having fun.

Sam Smith xo

A beautiful view!

Sam Smith